LIVING WITH
Your Higher Power

A WORKBOOK FOR STEPS 1–3

Created by James Hubal and Joanne Hubal

Based on material from *A Program for You: A Guide to the Big Book's* Design for Living* published by Hazelden Publishing

*BIG BOOK is a registered trademark of Alcoholics Anonymous World Services, Inc.; used here with permission of AAWS.

Hazelden Publishing
Center City, MN 55012
hazelden.org/bookstore

ISBN: 978-1-5683-8989-9

Editor's note:

Hazelden Publishing offers a variety of information on addiction
and related areas. Our publications do not necessarily represent
the Hazelden Betty Ford Foundation's programs, nor do they
officially speak for any Twelve Step organization.

The Twelve Steps and Twelve Traditions are reprinted and adapted
with permission of Alcoholics Anonymous World Services, Inc.
Permission to reprint and adapt the Twelve Steps does not mean
that Alcoholics Anonymous has reviewed or approved the contents of
this publication, nor that AA agrees with the views expressed herein.
The views expressed herein are solely those of the authors. AA is
a program of recovery from alcoholism. Use of the Twelve Steps in
connection with programs and activities that are patterned after AA,
but which address other problems, does not imply otherwise.

This workbook has been updated to include both third-
and fourth-edition page references to *Alcoholics Anonymous*.

Cover and interior design/typesetting: Sara Streifel, *Think Creative Design*
Developmental editor: Marc Olson
Editorial project manager: Victoria Tirrel

Contents

Introduction 1

My First Step: Knowing My Problem 3

Exercise 1   Being Out of Control: How Did It Feel? 3

Exercise 2   What Are Your Favorite Excuses? 4

Exercise 3   A Problem of the Body: A Physical Allergy 6

Exercise 4   Going to the Roots of Powerlessness 7

Exercise 5   Situations 9

Exercise 6   Patterns 11

Exercise 7   Video Screen 13

Exercise 8   A Problem of the Mind: A Mental Obsession 14

Exercise 9   Recognizing the Good and Bad Feelings 15

Exercise 10   Temptations 16

Exercise 11   Restless, Irritable, and Discontented 17

Exercise 12   The Alcohol and Drug Addiction Cycle 19

Exercise 13   Personal Alcohol and Drug Addiction Cycle 20

Exercise 14   Definitions 21

Exercise 15   How Is Bill W.'s Story Like Yours? 22

Exercise 16   The Big Book's Description of an Alcoholic 23

Your Second Step: The Solution 25

Exercise 1   True or False? 26

Exercise 2   A Picture of Insanity 27

Exercise 3   The Big Lie 27

Exercise 4   Tricks—Or, Insane Lies 28

Duplicating this page is illegal. Do not copy this material without written permission from the publisher.

iii

Exercise 5   **The Big Lie Landfill** 29

Exercise 6   **Why It's Essential to Believe In a Higher Power** 30

Exercise 7   **Coming to Terms with a Higher Power** 31

Exercise 8   **Belief and Faith** 32

Exercise 9   **Three Pertinent Ideas** 33

Step Three: Beginning My Plan of Action 35

Exercise 1   **"Self-Will Run Riot"** 35

Exercise 2   **When Behavior Conflicts with Values** 37

Exercise 3   **Turning It Over . . . and What's Ahead?** 38

Exercise 4   **What's Ahead?** 41

The Twelve Steps of Alcoholics Anonymous 42

The Twelve Traditions of Alcoholics Anonymous 43

Introduction

The book *Alcoholics Anonymous,* commonly known as the Big Book, is the basic text for the fellowship of Alcoholics Anonymous (AA). It was published in 1939 to show how the first one hundred or so AA members found recovery from alcoholism. The founders of AA were Bill W., a New York stockbroker, and Dr. Bob, an Akron, Ohio, physician. Bill W. wrote the Big Book with the help of Dr. Bob and the other early members. He wrote the first 164 pages in a specific order that has not been changed or reworded since 1939. He wrote these pages so that if other alcoholics read the suggestions for recovery and put them into practice in exactly the order Bill W. wrote them, they would find recovery too.

Since 1939 millions of alcoholics and, more recently, countless people suffering from other addictive behaviors have done just that—they have found recovery.

This program of recovery is not a philosophy or religion. It is a practical *design for living* that is summed up in the Twelve suggestions, or Steps, listed on pages 59–60 of the Big Book and on page 41 at the back of this workbook. If you aren't familiar with the Twelve Steps, you should read them through carefully now.

———

The first three Steps show us how we can build a working relationship with our Higher Power, or God *as we understand God.* Steps One, Two, and Three are covered in the Big Book from page xxiii [xxv, 4th ed.] to the bottom of page 63. The next four Steps—Steps Four through Seven—show us how we can better know and live at peace with ourselves. Steps Four, Five, Six, and Seven are covered in the Big Book from the last two lines of page 63 through the end of the second paragraph on page 76. Finally, the last five Steps—Steps Eight through Twelve—give us a design for living meaningful lives with other people and for continuing a daily program of recovery the rest of our lives. The Big Book covers these Steps from the third paragraph on page 76 to the end of page 103.

This workbook covers Steps One through Three and is the first of three workbooks covering all Twelve Steps. All three workbooks were written to help you study the Big Book and apply what it says. Much of the text in these workbooks is adapted from the book *A Program for You: A Guide to the Big Book's Design for Living*, written anonymously by two AA old-timers. You will benefit even more from these workbooks if you first read that book.*

While *A Program for You* is an optional supplement to these workbooks, a copy of the Big Book, *Alcoholics Anonymous*, is not—it is essential. Everything you need to know to be on the road to recovery from alcoholism (or another addiction) is in the Big Book. Anything else, including these workbooks, can only help you see what is already in the Big Book as you apply its suggestions in your life.

———

The Big Book and the fellowship of Alcoholics Anonymous are both concerned only with recovery from addiction to the drug alcohol. Neither the Big Book nor the fellowship makes any claim for what the suggestions in the Big Book will do for people other than alcoholics. Therefore, when referring to the Big Book or the AA fellowship, we will use the terms "alcohol" and "alcoholics."

Since the Big Book was written, many successful Twelve Step groups for recovery from other addictions and addictive behaviors have been established—Al-Anon, Cocaine Anonymous, Narcotics Anonymous, Overeaters Anonymous, and so on. While these groups publish their own literature, their basic program for recovery is not essentially different from the one described in AA's Big Book. In this workbook, when referring to recovery in general, or to you, the reader, we will use a variety of terms and references to include those who are not addicted specifically or exclusively to alcohol.

———

*A Program for You: A Guide to the Big Book's Design for Living is published by and available through Hazelden Publishing.

My First Step:
Knowing My Problem

There are three basic questions that you, while using the Big Book as your guide, must answer as part of your recovery from alcoholism or another addiction. They are:

1. What is the problem?

2. What is the solution?

3. What can I do to use that solution in my own life?

So the first thing you have to do is find out what the problem is.

Often an alcoholic or other addict who has not identified the problem says, "I haven't got a problem. I'm fine." Before taking Step One of the Twelve Steps, we *deny* there's a problem at all. But in the Big Book we learn that our lives are out of control because we are *powerless* over alcohol.

Here is the First Step in the AA Twelve Step program:

**"We admitted we were powerless over alcohol—
that our lives had become unmanageable."**

Let's start by looking at what it means to be powerless.

Exercise 1
Being Out of Control: How Did It Feel?

Think of a time when your life has been out of control. Maybe your car hit a slick or icy spot in the road, or a thunderstorm ruined a family picnic. Maybe you were called for jury duty when you wanted to do something else, or an illness or injury made it impossible for you to carry on with your life as usual. Whatever it was, think about it and then write or draw what happened in the space below. Be sure your words or drawing show how you *felt* when you were out of control.

The Big Book tells us that alcoholics are out of control—powerless—over alcohol, but as we've learned, they will usually say, "I'm fine."

Exercise 2
What Are Your Favorite Excuses?

What are some things you've said or thought to explain your use of alcohol or other drugs? Try to give at least two examples for each category.

1. To relatives:

2. To people at work:

3. To friends at a party or other social event:

4. To a romantic partner or spouse:

5. To yourself:

Here are some things alcoholics and other addicts typically say to convince others and themselves that they can control their drinking or using. Perhaps some of these were on your list.

- "I can stop anytime I want to."

- "I'm just going to try it."

- "I only get high to have a good time [or to loosen up, or for a release, or . . .]."

- "I can drink [or use] and drive."

- "You'd get high, too, if you had my problems."

- "Everyone drinks [or smokes pot, or pops pills . . .]."

- "You can't get addicted to weed [or beer, or ...]."

- "I'd know it if I was an addict [or a drunk]."

- "I can hold my liquor."

- "If I were a drunk [or an addict] I'd be on skid row [or in jail, or broke, or ...]."

If any of these fit you, you now know some of your favorite excuses for continuing to drink alcohol or use other drugs. It is important that you also know that these excuses are not the truth. They are just ways you may have unknowingly tricked yourself or tried to make others think you were in control and not powerless over alcohol or other drugs. It is more likely that *alcohol or other drugs have power over you.*

<table>
<tr><td>Exercise 3
A Problem of the Body: A Physical Allergy</td></tr>
</table>

> Now open the Big Book and read "The Doctor's Opinion" on pages xxiii–xxx [pages xxv–xxxii, 4th ed.].

On lines 10–23 of page xxiv [page xxvi, 4th ed.] is a description of how alcohol controls the alcoholic. Dr. William D. Silkworth, who treated alcoholics in the early days of AA, says that two parts of the alcoholic are controlled by alcohol. They are:

1. _____

2. _____

First, let's look at how alcohol and other drugs affect the body. Dr. Silkworth explains that alcoholism is an allergy to alcohol. What does the word *allergy* mean to you? (Feel free to use a dictionary or ask others for help in writing your definition.)

An allergy is _____

_____

_____

When Dr. Silkworth says that alcoholics have an allergy to alcohol, he means that their bodies can't handle it in a normal way. The same is true when someone is addicted to another drug. A lot of research shows that the brain chemistry of alcoholics and addicts eventually changes, so that alcohol and other drugs affect these people differently than nonalcoholics or nonaddicts.

This allergic reaction to alcohol or other drugs means that, as alcoholics or other addicts, we will at some point not be able to control our use after taking the first drink or hit—no matter what problems result or what we promised or decided otherwise. We are powerless over our use of alcohol or other drugs.

Exercise 4
Going to the Roots of Powerlessness

An alcoholic's or addict's powerlessness over mood-altering drugs shows itself in many ways. No two people react exactly the same, although there are often similar patterns. What all alcoholics and other addicts do have in common is that their use of alcohol or another drug is out of control, and they will continue to drink or use in spite of all the bad things that happen to them and others because of it.

Some of the different but equally out-of-control ways that alcoholics and addicts use substances are listed below. Put a check mark next to the ways that describe (or are close to describing) how you have used alcohol or other drugs. If some actions that pertain to you are not listed here, add them at the end of this list.

Alcoholics or addicts . . .

_____ will often drink or use when no one else is drinking or using.

_____ may drink or use any time of the day or night.

_____ hide the amount consumed or used.

_____ will use a drug of an unknown source or quality to get higher.

_____ bring their own booze or stash to a party when they know none will be there.

_____ will spend money that is needed for essentials (such as food) on alcohol or other drugs.

_____ will continue to drink or use when they're already drunk or high.

_____ will put themselves and others in danger by driving when high or drunk.

_____ will later deny or downplay foolish or dangerous behavior that occurred when they were drinking or high.

_____ will lie to friends and loved ones to protect their drinking or using.

_____ will continue to drink or use even though friends and loved ones are asking them to stop because of the harmful results.

List ways (that aren't on the list) you use or have used alcohol or other drugs.

Now, looking at the lists, write how your behavior may show that you are powerless over alcohol or drugs.

It is the allergy, described by Dr. Silkworth in the Big Book, that brings alcoholics or addicts to eventually crave and use more after the first drink (or snort or hit), in spite of their sincere conviction that this time they'll be able to drink or use like normal people. That is why the well-meaning advice to "just use more willpower" to quit drinking or using won't work.

Exercise 5
Situations

List three situations in which your drinking or other drug use was different from that of other people you were with. Tell where you were, who you were with, and how your behavior was different from that of the other people who were with you.

Situation #1

Where you were:

Who you were with:

How your behavior was different from others':

Situation #2

Where you were:

Who you were with:

How your behavior was different from others':

Situation #3

Where you were:

Who you were with:

How your behavior was different from others':

At the time each of these situations was happening, what were you thinking or wondering about the people who were *not* using drugs or drinking as you were?

How are you different from these people?

In the Big Book, the word *craving* always refers to your body—
the physical craving that comes *after* you've taken a drink or a drug.

Exercise 6
Patterns

1. What was your drinking or using pattern? (For example, "I drank frequently after work.")

Did you drink alcohol or use other drugs every day to maintain a certain feeling? Describe that feeling.

Did you binge, going out certain times of the week to get high or drunk? If so, when?

Or did you do something other than binge? (Explain)

2. Now compare your use of alcohol or other drugs to your use of a favorite (nonalcoholic) beverage or healthy snack. How is it different?

Whether the uncontrolled drinking and drug use is happening every day or every so often, alcoholics and other addicts have a craving that cannot be satisfied. It's a craving that kicks in *after* we put alcohol or another drug into our bodies.

People with a normal—not better, just different—reaction to alcohol or other drugs can stop drinking or using when they feel like it. An alcoholic or addict cannot. That's craving.

In the Big Book, Dr. Silkworth says that there are many different types of alcoholics, meaning there are many different ways alcoholics typically behave when drunk. Some people want to fight or argue; some start feeling sorry for themselves; some blame others for their problems. Some people withdraw and go off by themselves, sometimes abandoning family and friends. Others act out sexually or act like a clown.

Exercise 7
Video Screen

Pretend you're watching a video of some of the times you got drunk or high. Pretend that the box below is the video screen. Write in words or draw on the screen what your behavior would look like.

Is this—what you've written or drawn on the screen—how you behave when you *choose* your behavior (that is, when you're in control)?

☐ Yes ☐ No

Do you believe you had the ability to make a choice about stopping drinking or using before the moment you've shown on the screen?

☐ Yes   ☐ No

Many successful alcohol and other drug treatment programs are based on the idea of abstinence. As an alcoholic or addict, you'll never be able to drink or use other drugs safely for as long as you live.

Regardless of how alcoholics and addicts act when they're drunk or high, all of us share one thing: once we start drinking alcohol or using other drugs, it will eventually lead to more drinking or using until we are drunk, high, sick, or in trouble.

Look at lines 30–31 on page xxviii [page xxx, 4th ed.] of the Big Book.

The only relief or answer to the problem is entire _____.

Exercise 8
A Problem of the Mind: A Mental Obsession

Can you remember a time when you talked yourself into thinking you could drink alcohol or use drugs safely even after you'd repeatedly experienced serious problems due to your drinking or other drug use?

☐ Yes   ☐ No

What happened?

If alcoholics or other addicts know they can't drink or use safely, why does an alcoholic or addict take the first drink, the first snort, the first hit? Dr. Silkworth tells us that part of it is in the *mind*. Alcoholics and other addicts remember the good feelings they had the last time they used their drug of choice. Look at lines 30–31 on page xxvi [page xxviii, 4th ed.] of the Big Book. Dr. Silkworth says people drink

"essentially because _____

_____."

Exercise 9
Recognizing the Good and Bad Feelings

What feelings (good and bad) do you remember getting from using alcohol or other drugs?

Good Feelings	Bad Feelings
(For example: confident, relaxed, in control, sexy)	(For example: scared, ashamed, lonely, foolish)

Sometimes people's experiences with alcohol or other drugs can be very painful. There are lots of bad feelings and memories, but alcoholics' and addicts' brains trick them into remembering only the good feelings. It is important to be aware of what these good feelings are, because the false idea that you can have them again, but without the harmful consequences this time, is how your addicted mind gets you to take the first drink or drug. After that, craving takes over.

Exercise 10
Temptations

Let's take this a step further. In addition to remembering only the good feelings that came from past drinking or other drug use, there are other triggers and experiences that might encourage alcoholics or addicts to think they need to drink alcohol or use other drugs.

Describe briefly how each of the following items might play a part in getting you to think you need to drink alcohol or use other drugs.

Being with certain people:

Being at a certain place:

Hearing a special song or type of music:

Eating certain types of food:

A particular time of day:

Participating in certain activities:

Having something happen (name this) that always causes stress:

Other:

Because they are linked to the experience of **drinking or using**, these people, places, events, activities, situations, and special feelings that you just described are especially appealing to you as an alcoholic or addict. In the Big Book on page xxvi [page xxviii, 4th ed.], lines 34–35, Dr. Silkworth says when practicing alcoholics are not drinking,

they feel _____, _____, and _____.

Exercise 11
Restless, Irritable, and Discontented

Think about some typical situations where you have been restless, irritable, or discontented. What kinds of thoughts did you have in these situations? What feelings usually arose from these thoughts? What were some of the behaviors that regularly resulted from these thoughts and feelings?

Write down some examples of regular patterns of thoughts, feelings, and behaviors that have led you to want to drink or use, or to actually drink or use other drugs.

Restless

Thoughts: _____

Feelings: _____

Behaviors: _____

Irritable

Thoughts: _____

Feelings: _____

Behaviors: _____

Discontented

Thoughts: _____

Feelings: _____

Behaviors: _____

It can work like this:

1. You feel <u>restless, irritable,</u> or <u>discontented</u>.
2. You <u>remember the good feelings</u> alcohol or drugs brought in the past. The thought that you can drink or use like normal people becomes an obsession.
3. This overpowering idea <u>(obsession)</u> convinces your mind that you can drink or use without negative consequences, and leads you to put yourself in situations where drinking or using is possible or likely. You do this in spite of past problems related to your alcohol or drug use.
4. You <u>take a drink or use drugs</u>. At that point, because of the allergic reaction, you crave more alcohol or drugs. So you continue drinking or using.

5. What follows is a drug or drinking spree that causes your behavior to go <u>out of control</u>.

6. Afterward, you <u>feel sorry</u> (remorseful).

7. You <u>make a promise</u> (resolution) never to drink alcohol or use other drugs again.

When this happens repeatedly, it becomes the Alcohol and Drug Addiction Cycle.

Exercise 12
The Alcohol and Drug Addiction Cycle

Look at the seven numbered items you just read above, and use the underlined words to fill in the seven stages of the Alcohol and Drug Addiction Cycle on the diagram below.

Now you're ready to complete a personal Alcohol and Drug Addiction Cycle diagram. Using the same seven categories as in the previous diagram, add examples from your life to show how the cycle could lead you to drink or use other drugs. Remember what you learned in the previous exercises about your drinking and using behavior as you complete the diagram below.

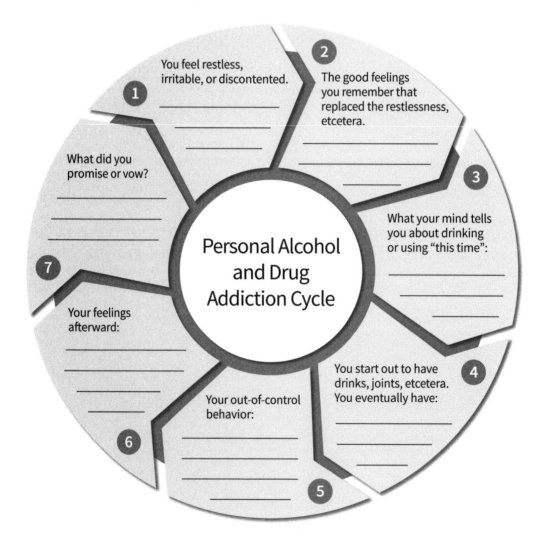

Now look at page xxvii [page xxix, 4th ed.], lines 7–9, of the Big Book. Dr. Silkworth states that an alcoholic repeats the drinking cycle over and over, unless the person "can experience an _____ _____ _____." Since alcoholics and addicts can't do anything about their allergy to alcohol or other drugs—the illness of the body—recovery will have to come *through the mind*. But before we move ahead with the Steps, let's take a moment to review some key terms.

Exercise 14
Definitions

Define in your own words:

1. Obsession

2. Allergy

3. Craving

4. Unmanageable

5. Remorseful

6. Powerless

7. Choice

Chapter 1 of the Big Book tells Bill W.'s story. His experience shows us that the problem of alcoholism has a practical solution that can be used by ordinary people.

> Read Bill W.'s story (pages 1–16 of the Big Book). Pay special attention to the first part, where he describes the misery and hopelessness of his situation. Bill's experiences show how his condition involved his whole self: body, mind, and spirit. It is easy for most alcoholics and other addicts to identify with some part of Bill's story.

Exercise 15
How Is Bill W.'s Story Like Yours?

Using the chart on the next page, describe how Bill W.'s story is like, or not like, your own experience with alcohol or other drugs.

Bill's Experience	Your Experience
Drinking	Drinking (or using)
With money	With money
With family	With family
On the job	On the job
With friends	With friends

Exercise 16
The Big Book's Description of an Alcoholic

In the Big Book read the description of an alcoholic, from line 8 of page 21 through line 3 of page 25.

Duplicating this page is illegal. Do not copy this material without written permission from the publisher.

My First Step: Knowing My Problem   23

List each part of that description that applies to your own alcohol or drug use. (Examples: "I eventually lost all control of my liquor or drug consumption." "Even my most powerful desire to stop drinking or using didn't work." "I also thought, *This time it won't burn me.*")

1. _____

2. _____

3. _____

4. _____

5. _____

(List as many more as needed on a separate sheet.)

If you can't drink or use drugs because of your body, but you can't quit drinking or using drugs because of your mind, then you are powerless over alcohol and other drugs. Seeing this and realizing its truth is your First Step in your recovery. It means you understand the problem.

> If you are unsure whether you have taken a First Step, go back to "The Doctor's Opinion" beginning on page xxiii [page xxv, 4th ed.] of the Big Book and read it again, slowly and carefully, continuing through Bill W.'s story to the end of page 16. As you read, review what you've written or drawn in the previous exercises, and make changes and additions as needed.

Your Second Step:
The Solution

The important thing about Bill W.'s story, about *your* story, is that, like Bill, you don't have to remain helpless and miserable. What happened to Bill can happen to you. Awareness of what the problem is can lead to the solution. Step Two is that solution.

Here is the Second Step in the AA Twelve Step program:

**"Came to believe that a Power greater than
ourselves could restore us to sanity."**

In order to understand Step Two, you must first understand these four ideas:

1. Spiritual experience
2. Sanity and insanity
3. Higher Power
4. Belief and faith

First, let's discuss *spiritual experience*. This idea is central to your recovery.

> Stop now and read chapter 2 of the Big Book, "There Is a Solution," pages 17–29, and read Appendix II, pages 569–570 [pages 567–568, 4th ed.].
>
> The phrase *spiritual experiences* is first mentioned on **page 25** of the Big Book and is explained in detail in Appendix II.

After reading the descriptions of "spiritual experience" in the Big Book, circle either *T* or *F* (for *true* or *false*) after each of the following statements.

1. A spiritual experience must be sudden and spectacular. T F

2. By using self-discipline, an alcoholic can get the same results that a spiritual experience will give. T F

3. For many, having a spiritual experience means tapping inner resources, which they think of as a Power greater than themselves. T F

4. Even if you close your mind to spiritual ideas, you can recover from alcoholism. T F

5. *Change* is what a spiritual experience is all about. T F

Now look at the answers you circled. Explain here why you think statements 1, 2, and 4 would not be true.

The Big Book contains many stories about the "insanity" alcoholics experience. Remember, Step Two says "that a Power greater than ourselves could restore us to *sanity*." (Italics added.) This Step clearly says that sanity is something alcoholics and other addicts (who are not in recovery) are missing. That can only mean that what you experience, as a practicing alcoholic or addict, is *insanity*.

Exercise 2
A Picture of Insanity

Describe in words or draw a picture to show what you think of when you hear the word *insanity*.

The author of the Big Book, Bill W., may have been thinking about insanity in just a little different way. The Big Book describes the insanity that takes place *before* an alcoholic takes a drink or the addict uses drugs.

> Now stop and read chapter 3, "More about Alcoholism," pages 30–43 of the Big Book.

Exercise 3
The Big Lie

Look again at page 30 of the Big Book. What is the Big Lie that alcoholics tell themselves, described in paragraph 1?

This lie ("I'll be able to drink alcohol or use drugs like other people") is the root of the alcoholic's and addict's insane thinking. The lie comes into our minds *not* while we are drinking alcohol or using drugs and are controlled by our allergy. The Big Lie is the part of our disorder that's in our minds when we're *not using.*

To avoid facing the fact that we can't drink alcohol or use drugs like other people, we'll inevitably try to come up with what feel like well-thought-out ways to do so.

This Big Lie becomes our *obsession,*
or the idea that replaces all others.

Exercise 4
Tricks—or, Insane Lies

In the Big Book read the paragraph beginning on line 17 of page 31. There you'll find a list of tricks alcoholics typically use to try to control their drinking on their own—such as drinking beer only, and so on. Once you've read the entire list, write below some methods you've tried. If your favorite methods are not listed on page 31 of the Big Book, add your own to the list. (If alcohol isn't your drug of choice, consider your behavior with other drugs.)

1. _____

2. _____

3. _____

4. _____

5. _____

6. _____

7. _____

8. _____

Remember, acting on these insane lies is what leads us to trouble. As an alcoholic or other addict, you've more than likely lost things that are important to you: family, job, driver's license, and more.

Exercise 5
The Big Lie Landfill

What follows is a drawing called the Big Lie Landfill—it is simply a dump. On the bags in the dump, write the names of people and things you've lost because you believed the lie that you could drink alcohol or use drugs safely. Add more bags if you need to.

Big Lie Landfill

Believing the Big Lie that you can drink alcohol or use drugs like other people is your insanity. And the Big Book makes it clear on page 39, lines 7–9, that as an alcoholic, you will be *"absolutely unable to stop drinking on the basis of* _____."

The Big Book states at the bottom of page 43 that "the alcoholic at certain times has no effective mental defense against the first drink." Instead, the ability to keep from taking that first drink "must come from a Higher Power."

Exercise 6
Why It's Essential to Believe In a Higher Power

Whether or not you're a religious person, you probably have an idea of what "Higher Power" means. Draw or write below what you imagine when you think about a Higher Power.

Now stop and read chapter 4 of the Big Book, "We Agnostics," pages 44–57. Chapter 4 explains why a spiritual experience can happen even to an atheist or agnostic or someone with little or no religious experience. Chapter 4 goes on to say that it isn't hard or unusual to believe in a Higher Power. In fact, the chapter makes it clear that recovery always includes the spiritual experience of coming to trust a Higher Power.

Exercise 7
Coming to Terms with a Higher Power

Every person has a different image of a Higher Power, and every person has a unique experience with religion or spiritual ideas. If there are experiences in your past or things you believe that make you think it would be hard (or even impossible) for you to believe in a Higher Power, write them here.

Did reading chapter 4 of the Big Book change your feelings at all?

☐ Yes   ☐ No

If so, how? If not. Why not?

How does the Big Book define *Higher Power*? Put it in your own words.

Belief and Faith

The Big Book states on page 45, lines 13–15, that its "main object is to enable you to find a Power greater than yourself which will solve your problem." On page 47, lines 15–16, what is the important question you need to ask yourself?

Copy it here: _____

_____

_____

Belief comes *before* an action or decision; faith comes afterward, as the result of an action or decision. Here's an example from *A Program for You:*

Suppose you've just moved to a new town where you don't know anyone. One day your car begins to give you trouble, so you decide you'd better get it fixed. You knock on your neighbor's door, introduce yourself, and ask her, "Do you know of a good mechanic in town?" She recommends a fellow named Mel and tells you, "Mel does good work. I've been taking my car to him for years." So you decide to take your car to Mel.

Now, you've never met Mel, and you've only known the person who recommended him for about five minutes. But you decide to take your car to Mel because you believe that your neighbor is telling the truth and that she has reasonably good judgment when it comes to car mechanics. For the moment, at least, you also believe that Mel probably does do good work. You don't have any *faith* in Mel yet—only *belief*. But this belief is enough for you to make a decision and take action.

Let's say that Mel works on your car, fixes it correctly and promptly, and charges a fair price. You are pleased with his work, so when you have another problem with your car a year or so later, you take it back to him for repair. This time, though, you're going back to Mel on faith, not just on belief. You have faith that he can fix your car well, based on your actual experience.

Your *faith* could only happen because of your initial *willingness* to believe and the action you took based on that belief.

For some of us there is confusion about the idea of "belief" and "faith." The Big Book asks you to *believe* in a Power greater than yourself.

Write an example from your own life of some person, idea, or thing that you first *believed* in, and later had *faith* in.

First the belief, then the action, then faith. There are many different ways faith can be acquired. The Big Book is clear about this: people of just about all religions and spiritual affiliations will find nothing in the AA fellowship that contradicts their own beliefs. Deep down in every person is a basic idea of a Higher Power. Your belief that this Higher Power can restore you to sanity will be the foundation for your plan of action for recovery that is contained in Steps Three through Twelve. *Putting that plan into practice will bring you the spiritual experience that changes your belief into faith.*

Exercise 9
Three Pertinent Ideas

> Now slowly and carefully read and reread the beginning of chapter 5, "How it Works," from page 58 through line 20 on page 60.

Look again at lines 13–20 on page 60 of the Big Book. Write down the three pertinent ideas that the Big Book says should be clear to you at this point. (Substitute *addicts* for *alcoholics* and *addiction* for *alcoholism* as needed.)

a. _____

_____

b. _____

_____

c. _____

_____

> If you're convinced that these three ideas apply to you so far, proceed with Step Three. If not, go back to the Big Book and reread whatever you're not convinced of and, if need be, add to or change what you've written so far.

Step Three:
Beginning My Plan of Action

Here is the Third Step in the AA Twelve Step program:

**"Made a decision to turn our will and our lives over
to the care of God as we understood Him."***

▶ Stop now and read the Big Book from page 60, line 21 through
line 31 on page 63. This section describes Step Three.

Exercise 1
"Self-Will Run Riot"

Fill in the blank: Near the bottom of page 60, the Big Book says that, until we're convinced that a life run on _____ won't be a success; we're like an actor who wants to run the whole show.

Who are the people you have tried to control? Take a separate sheet of paper and write each person's name across the top of the page. Beneath each person's name, write what you tried to get that person to do. In other words, how have you tried to run each person's life?

Who plays the other characters in your "show"? On the next page, write a name inside each circle (add more circles as needed).

---

*Although the Big Book, written in the late 1930s, refers to "God" as "Him," no deliberate gender preference was intended by the author. The word *Her* or simply *God,* depending on your preference, can be substituted for *Him.*

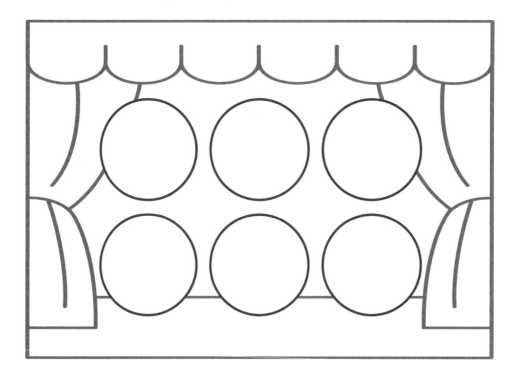

Fill in the blanks: Near the top of page 62 in the Big Book, we are told that _____ is at the root of our problems, and that "driven by a hundred forms of _____, _____, _____, and _____," we hurt others.

We are also told near the bottom of page 62 (last paragraph) that in order to reduce this *self*-centeredness, we must quit playing _____ and let _____ be the Director.

In other words, God, *as you understand God,* is the real Director of your life and your recovery. What gets in the way is *self*-will. Will is nothing more than your mind and your thinking. Your will is the thing up in your head that tells you what to do and, properly used, is aligned with God's will so that God can be your Director.

In the middle of page 62, the Big Book says that an alcoholic or other addict "is an extreme example of *self-will run riot.*" (Italics added.) This means we're so driven by self-will that even though we have "moral and philosophical convictions galore," we can't live up to them—we continue to hurt ourselves and others.

When Behavior Conflicts with Values

Think of an incident directly related to your drinking or drug use when your behavior was in conflict with your values, and answer these questions:

What did you do that was in conflict with your values?

Which of your values did you go against?

What was your explanation then?

How do you explain it now?

How might you act differently now if God—your Higher Power—were your guide?

Turning It Over . . . and What's Ahead?

The idea of turning over your will and life to a Higher Power can be a very frightening one. Think about what areas of your life will be the hardest to turn over to a Higher Power.

In the list that follows, put a *1* by the most difficult thing to turn over. Then continue ranking things from the most difficult to the least difficult thing to turn over. If there is anything in your life more difficult to turn over than what's listed here, you may add to or substitute for the items below.

_____ self-serving sexual gratification

_____ the need to be special, unique, or different

_____ friends who drink or use

_____ the need to be nothing but the best

_____ the need to have things always go my way

_____ the idea that I can drink or use other drugs normally

_____ self-pity

_____ resentments over past harm

_____ the need for control over family members, co-workers, or friends

_____ the high, and all the rituals for getting there

_____ (other) _____

_____ (other) _____

Now, starting with the areas of your life (from the preceding list) that you think will be the hardest to turn over to a Higher Power, describe below, in a few words, what you're afraid will happen if you turn each of these over.

This fear of giving your will and life to a Higher Power is not unusual. Yet as alcoholics or addicts, we've already given our will and lives to something—alcohol or another drug. It often determined where we went, who we associated with, who we slept with, and how we spent our money. We have a disease of the body and mind that will end in insanity or death unless we make the decision required in Step Three.

Compared to turning our lives over to alcohol or another drug, deciding to turn our will and life over to a Higher Power should be far less frightening. And Step Three only asks us to *make the decision* to turn our will and life over to our Higher Power. The actual turning over of our will and life occurs naturally in the course of working the next eight Steps.

Turn in the Big Book to page 25, and read the passage on lines 25–32. What are your choices? Write them on the diagram below.

What's Ahead?

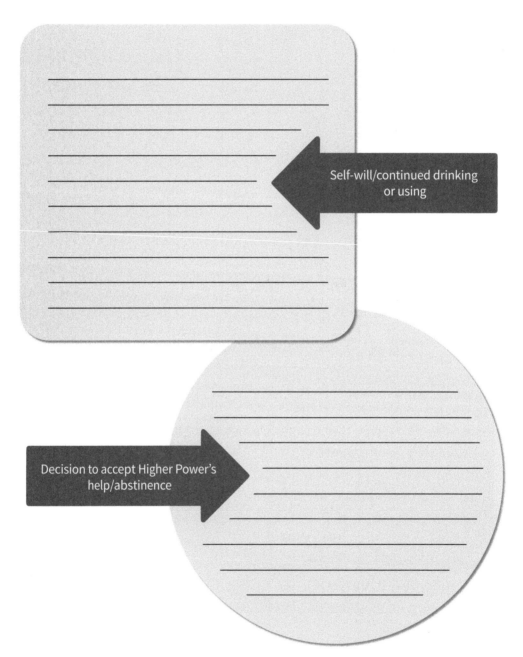

Self-will/continued drinking or using

Decision to accept Higher Power's help/abstinence

▶ Read the prayer on page 64, lines 14–20, in your Big Book.

Write out in your own words what this prayer means to you.

If possible, share what you've written aloud with someone you trust—your sponsor, counselor, or an understanding friend or relative. Otherwise say what you've written to yourself and your Higher Power.

In taking the Third Step, as the Big Book says on page 62, lines 31–33, you put in place "*the keystone of the new and triumphant arch through which [you will pass] to freedom.*" (Italics added.)

You are now ready for your Fourth Step.

The Twelve Steps of Alcoholics Anonymous*

1. We admitted we were powerless over alcohol—that our lives had become unmanageable.

2. Came to believe that a Power greater than ourselves could restore us to sanity.

3. Made a decision to turn our will and our lives over to the care of God *as we understood Him.*

4. Made a searching and fearless moral inventory of ourselves.

5. Admitted to God, to ourselves, and to another human being the exact nature of our wrongs.

6. Were entirely ready to have God remove all these defects of character.

7. Humbly asked Him to remove our shortcomings.

8. Made a list of all persons we had harmed, and became willing to make amends to them all.

9. Made direct amends to such people wherever possible, except when to do so would injure them or others.

10. Continued to take personal inventory and when we were wrong promptly admitted it.

11. Sought through prayer and meditation to improve our conscious contact with God *as we understood Him,* praying only for knowledge of His will for us and the power to carry that out.

12. Having had a spiritual awakening as the result of these steps, we tried to carry this message to alcoholics, and to practice these principles in all our affairs.

---

*The Twelve Steps of AA are taken from *Alcoholics Anonymous,* 3rd and 4th editions, published by A.A. World Services, Inc., New York, N.Y., 59–60. Reprinted with permission of A.A. World Services, Inc.

The Twelve Traditions of Alcoholics Anonymous*

1. Our common welfare should come first; personal recovery depends upon A.A. unity.

2. For our group purpose there is but one ultimate authority—a loving God as He may express Himself in our group conscience. Our leaders are but trusted servants; they do not govern.

3. The only requirement for A.A. membership is a desire to stop drinking.

4. Each group should be autonomous except in matters affecting other groups or A.A. as a whole.

5. Each group has but one primary purpose—to carry its message to the alcoholic who still suffers.

6. An A.A. group ought never endorse, finance or lend the A.A. name to any related facility or outside enterprise, lest problems of money, property and prestige divert us from our primary purpose.

7. Every A.A. group ought to be fully self-supporting, declining outside contributions.

8. Alcoholics Anonymous should remain forever nonprofessional, but our service centers may employ special workers.

9. A.A., as such, ought never be organized; but we may create service boards or committees directly responsible to those they serve.

10. Alcoholics Anonymous has no opinion on outside issues; hence the A.A. name ought never be drawn into public controversy.

11. Our public relations policy is based on attraction rather than promotion; we need always maintain personal anonymity at the level of press, radio, and films.

12. Anonymity is the spiritual foundation of all our Traditions, ever reminding us to place principles before personalities.

---

*The Twelve Traditions of AA are taken from *Alcoholics Anonymous,* 3rd ed., published by A.A. World Services, Inc., New York, NY, 564 [page 562, 4th ed.]. Reprinted with permission of A.A. World Services, Inc.

About the Authors

Writers and educators James and Joanne Hubal bring to their work years of training and experience in various areas of expertise, including the field of addiction treatment. Joanne Hubal has been a writer, teacher, and cartoonist. She specializes in education and humor writing. James Hubal has developed and modified curriculum materials for schools throughout the country.

Since they were first published in 1991, the Hubals' *Living With...* workbooks, adapted from the material written in *A Program for You: A Guide to the Big Book's Design for Living,* have helped hundreds of thousands of recovering people engage and incorporate the Twelve Steps in their lives of healing and recovery.

———

About Hazelden Publishing

As part of the Hazelden Betty Ford Foundation, Hazelden Publishing offers both cutting-edge educational resources and inspirational books. Our print and digital works help guide individuals in treatment and recovery, and their loved ones. Professionals who work to prevent and treat addiction also turn to Hazelden Publishing for evidence-based curricula; digital content solutions; and videos for use in schools, treatment and correctional programs, and community settings. We also offer training for implementation of our curricula.

Through published and digital works, Hazelden Publishing extends the reach of healing and hope to individuals, families, and communities affected by addiction and related issues.

For more information about Hazelden publications,
please call **800-328-9000**
or visit us online at **hazelden.org/bookstore**.

Also in This Series

A Program for You: A Guide to the Big Book's Design for Living

This celebration of the basic text of Twelve Step recovery breathes new life into the Big Book's timeless wisdom. Thoroughly annotated, written with down-to-earth humor and simplicity, and providing a contemporary context for understanding, *A Program for You* helps us experience the same path of renewal that Bill W. and the first one hundred AA members did.

Item 5122 · 192 pages

Living with Yourself: A Workbook for Steps 4–7

This workbook features information to reinforce important points in *A Program for You* and includes exercises for self-examination and disclosure. Clear discussions of Steps 4–7 and probing questions offer a guide to personal insight and reflection.

Item 5422 · 64 pages

Living with Others: A Workbook for Steps 8–12

This workbook features information to reinforce important points in *A Program for You* and includes exercises for self-examination and disclosure. Clear discussions of Steps 8–12 and probing questions offer a guide to personal insight and reflection.

Item 5423 · 52 pages

Other Titles That May Interest You

A Gentle Path through the Twelve Steps
By Patrick Carnes

Renowned addiction expert and best-selling author Patrick Carnes, PhD, brings readers a personal portal to the wisdom of the Twelve Steps.

Item 2558 · 340 pages

Twelve Step Pamphlet Collection

Used by patients in recovery centers throughout the nation, these easy-to-read editions are a sure way to gain a basic, and yet thorough, understanding of the significance of each Step.

Item 1455 · 12 Pamphlets

Twenty-Four Hours a Day

A mainstay in recovery literature, "the little black book—*Twenty-Four Hours a Day*"—is the first and foremost meditation book for anyone practicing the Twelve Steps of AA. Millions of copies sold.

Item 1050 · 400 pages

Coming Soon

How We Heal

A diverse and inclusive meditation book for people with co-occurring sexual trauma and substance use disorders, this unique title brings together many individual voices to create a symphony of survivors all saying the same thing: you are not alone.